baking
favourites

THE AUSTRALIAN
Women's Weekly

CONTENTS

AUSTRALIAN CUP AND
SPOON MEASUREMENTS
ARE METRIC. A
CONVERSION CHART
APPEARS ON PAGE 77.

The pleasure of home-made cakes, biscuits and slices is not just in the eating, it's also in the preparation and baking and the looks of delight on the faces of your appreciative audience as they wait for your creation to come out of the oven. There's something magical about mixing together a few simple ingredients – butter, sugar, eggs, flour – and watching them turn into something wonderful.

Pamela Clark

Food Director

TRADITIONAL SHORTBREAD

prep + cook time 1 hour **makes** 24

250g butter, softened
⅓ cup (75g) caster sugar
1 tablespoon water
2 cups (300g) plain flour
½ cup (100g) rice flour
2 tablespoons white sugar

1 Preheat oven to 160°C/140°C fan-forced.
Grease oven trays.
2 Beat butter and caster sugar in medium
bowl with electric mixer until light and fluffy; stir
in the water and sifted flours, in two batches.
Knead on floured surface until smooth.
3 Divide mixture in half; shape each on
separate trays into 20cm rounds. Mark each
round into 12 wedges; prick with fork. Pinch
edges of rounds with fingers; sprinkle with
white sugar.
4 Bake about 40 minutes; stand 5 minutes.
Using sharp knife, cut into wedges along
marked lines. Cool on trays.
Store in an airtight container for up to a week.

BISCUITS

HONEY JUMBLES

prep + cook time 25 minutes (+ refrigeration) makes 40

60g butter
½ cup (110g) firmly packed brown sugar
¾ cup (270g) golden syrup
1 egg, beaten lightly
2½ cups (375g) plain flour
½ cup (75g) self-raising flour
½ teaspoon bicarbonate of soda
1 teaspoon ground cinnamon
½ teaspoon ground clove
2 teaspoons ground ginger
1 teaspoon mixed spice
glacé icing
1 egg white
1½ cups (240g) icing sugar
2 teaspoons plain flour
1 tablespoon lemon juice, approximately
pink food colouring

1 Preheat oven to 160°C/140°C fan-forced. Grease oven trays.

2 Combine butter, sugar and syrup in medium saucepan; stir over low heat until sugar dissolves. Cool 10 minutes. Transfer mixture to large bowl; stir in egg and sifted dry ingredients, in two batches. Knead dough on floured surface until dough loses its stickiness, cover; refrigerate 30 minutes.

3 Divide dough into 8 portions. Roll each portion into a 2cm-thick sausage; cut each sausage into five 6cm lengths. Place about 3cm apart on oven trays; round ends with lightly floured fingers, flatten slightly.

4 Bake about 15 minutes; cool on trays.

5 Make glacé icing.

6 Spread jumbles with pink and white icing.

glacé icing Beat egg white lightly in small bowl; gradually stir in sifted icing sugar and flour, then enough juice to make icing spreadable. Place half the mixture in another small bowl; tint lightly with colouring. Keep icings covered with a damp tea towel while in use to stop from drying out.

Store in an airtight container for up to a week.

peanut butter cookies

VANILLA KISSES

prep + cook time **25 minutes** makes **20**

125g butter, softened
½ cup (110g) caster sugar
1 egg
⅓ cup (50g) plain flour
¼ cup (35g) self-raising flour
⅔ cup (100g) cornflour
¼ cup (30g) custard powder
vienna cream
60g butter, softened
½ teaspoon vanilla extract
¾ cup (120g) icing sugar
2 teaspoons milk

1 Preheat oven to 200°C/180°C fan-forced. Grease oven trays; line with baking paper.
2 Beat butter, sugar and egg in small bowl with electric mixer until light and fluffy. Stir in sifted dry ingredients, in two batches.
3 Spoon mixture into piping bag fitted with 1cm-fluted tube. Pipe 3cm rosettes about 3cm apart on trays. Bake about 10 minutes; cool on trays.
4 Meanwhile, make vienna cream. Sandwich biscuits with vienna cream.
vienna cream Beat butter and extract in small bowl with electric mixer until as white as possible; gradually beat in sifted icing sugar and milk, in two batches.
Store in an airtight container for up to a week.

PEANUT BUTTER COOKIES

prep + cook time **25 minutes** makes **30**

125g butter, softened
¼ cup (70g) crunchy peanut butter
¾ cup (165g) firmly packed brown sugar
1 egg
1½ cups (225g) plain flour
½ teaspoon bicarbonate of soda
½ cup (70g) roasted unsalted peanuts, chopped coarsely

1 Preheat oven to 180°C/160°C fan-forced. Grease oven trays; line with baking paper.
2 Beat butter, peanut butter, sugar and egg in small bowl with electric mixer until smooth; do not over-mix. Transfer mixture to medium bowl; stir in sifted flour and soda, then nuts.
3 Roll level tablespoons of mixture into balls; place 5cm apart on trays, flatten with floured fork. Bake about 12 minutes; cool on trays.
Store in an airtight container for up to a week.

vanilla kisses

white chocolate and macadamia cookies

WHITE CHOCOLATE AND MACADAMIA COOKIES

prep + cook time **20 minutes** makes **24**

1½ cups (225g) plain flour
½ teaspoon bicarbonate of soda
¼ cup (55g) caster sugar
¹/₃ cup (75g) firmly packed brown sugar
125g butter, melted
½ teaspoon vanilla extract
1 egg
180g white eating chocolate,
    chopped coarsely
¾ cup (105g) roasted macadamias,
    chopped coarsely

1 Preheat oven to 200°C/180°C fan-forced.
Grease oven trays; line with baking paper.
2 Sift flour, soda and sugars into large bowl.
Stir in butter, extract and egg, then chocolate
and nuts.
3 Drop rounded tablespoons of mixture,
5cm apart on trays. Bake about 10 minutes.
Cool on trays.
Store in an airtight container for up to a week.

anzac biscuits

ANZAC BISCUITS

prep + cook time **35 minutes** makes **25**

1 cup (90g) rolled oats
1 cup (150g) plain flour
1 cup (220g) firmly packed brown sugar
½ cup (40g) desiccated coconut
125g butter
2 tablespoons golden syrup
1 tablespoon water
½ teaspoon bicarbonate of soda

1 Preheat oven to 160°C/140°C fan-forced.
Grease oven trays; line with baking paper.
2 Combine oats, sifted flour, sugar and
coconut in large bowl. Combine butter, syrup
and the water in small saucepan; stir over
low heat until smooth, stir in soda. Stir into
dry ingredients.
3 Roll level tablespoons of mixture into balls;
place about 5cm apart on trays, flatten slightly.
Bake about 20 minutes; cool on trays.
Store in an airtight container for up to a week.

PISTACHIO AND CRANBERRY BISCOTTI

prep + cook time **1 hour (+ refrigeration and cooling)**
makes **60**

60g unsalted butter, softened
1 teaspoon vanilla extract
1 cup (220g) caster sugar
2 eggs
1¾ cups (260g) plain flour
½ teaspoon bicarbonate of soda
1 cup (130g) dried cranberries
¾ cup (110g) coarsely chopped roasted pistachios
1 egg, extra
1 tablespoon water
2 tablespoons caster sugar, extra

1 Beat butter, extract and sugar in medium bowl until combined. Beat in eggs, one at a time. Stir in sifted flour and soda, then cranberries and nuts. Cover dough; refrigerate 1 hour.

2 Preheat oven to 180°C/160°C fan-forced. Grease oven tray.

3 Knead dough on floured surface until smooth but still sticky. Halve dough; shape each half into 30cm log. Place logs on oven tray.

4 Combine extra egg with the water in small bowl. Brush egg mixture over logs; sprinkle with extra sugar. Bake about 20 minutes or until firm; cool 3 hours or overnight.

5 Preheat oven to 160°C/140°C fan-forced.

6 Using serrated knife, cut logs diagonally into 1cm slices. Place slices on ungreased oven trays. Bake about 15 minutes or until dry and crisp, turning halfway through baking time; cool on wire racks.

Store **in an airtight container for up to two weeks.**

chocolate chip cookies

CHOCOLATE CHIP COOKIES

prep + cook time 40 minutes (+ refrigeration) makes 40

250g butter, softened
1 teaspoon vanilla extract
¾ cup (165g) caster sugar
¾ cup (165g) firmly packed brown sugar
1 egg
2¼ cups (335g) plain flour
1 teaspoon bicarbonate of soda
375g dark chocolate Melts, chopped coarsely

1 Preheat oven to 180°C/160°C fan-forced.
Grease oven trays; line with baking paper.
2 Beat butter, extract, sugars and egg in small
bowl with electric mixer until light and fluffy.
Transfer mixture to large bowl; stir in sifted flour
and soda, in two batches. Stir in chocolate,
cover; refrigerate 1 hour.
3 Roll level tablespoons of mixture into balls;
place about 3cm apart on trays. Bake about
12 minutes; cool on trays.

Store in an airtight container for up to a week.

variations

Dark chocolate can be replaced with either milk or
white chocolate.

For choc-nut cookies, replace a third of the chocolate
with roasted chopped nuts such as hazelnuts, walnuts
or pecans.

gingernuts

GINGERNUTS

prep + cook time 25 minutes makes 32

90g butter
$^1/_3$ cup (75g) firmly packed brown sugar
$^1/_3$ cup (115g) golden syrup
$1^1/_3$ cup (200g) plain flour
¾ teaspoon bicarbonate of soda
1 tablespoon ground ginger
1 teaspoon ground cinnamon
¼ teaspoon ground cloves

1 Preheat oven to 180°C/160°C fan-forced.
Grease oven trays.
2 Combine butter, sugar and syrup in medium
saucepan; stir over low heat until smooth.
Remove from heat; stir in sifted dry ingredients.
Cool 10 minutes.
3 Roll rounded teaspoons of mixture into balls.
Place about 3cm apart on trays; flatten slightly.
Bake about 10 minutes; cool on trays.
Store in an airtight container for up to a week.

PINK MACAROONS

prep + cook time **35 minutes (+ standing)** makes **18**

3 egg whites
2 tablespoons caster sugar
pink food colouring
1¼ cups (200g) icing sugar
1 cup (120g) ground almonds
2 tablespoons icing sugar, extra
white chocolate ganache
100g white eating chocolate,
    chopped coarsely
2 tablespoons thickened cream

1 Make white chocolate ganache.
2 Grease oven trays; line with baking paper.
3 Beat egg whites in small bowl with electric mixer until soft peaks form. Add sugar and food colouring, beat until sugar dissolves. Transfer mixture to large bowl. Fold in sifted icing sugar and ground almonds, in two batches.
4 Spoon mixture into large piping bag fitted with 1.5cm plain tube. Pipe 36 x 4cm rounds, 2cm apart, onto trays. Tap trays on bench so macaroons spread slightly. Dust with sifted extra icing sugar; stand 15 minutes.
5 Preheat oven to 150°C/130°C fan-forced.
6 Bake macaroons about 20 minutes. Stand 5 minutes; transfer to wire rack to cool.
7 Sandwich macaroons with ganache. Dust with a little sifted icing sugar, if desired.
white chocolate ganache Stir chocolate and cream in small saucepan over low heat until smooth. Transfer mixture to small bowl. Cover; refrigerate until mixture is spreadable.

Store **unfilled macaroons an airtight container for up to a week. Filled macaroons are best eaten on the day they are made.**

mini florentines

MINI FLORENTINES

prep + cook time **15 minutes** makes **25**

¾ cup (120g) sultanas
2 cups (80g) corn flakes
¾ cup (60g) roasted flaked almonds
½ cup (100g) red glacé cherries
²/₃ cup (160ml) sweetened condensed milk
60g white eating chocolate, melted
60g dark eating chocolate, melted

1 Preheat oven to 180°C/160°C fan-forced.
Grease oven trays; line with baking paper.
2 Combine sultanas, corn flakes, nuts, cherries
and condensed milk in medium bowl.
3 Drop level tablespoons of mixture about 5cm
apart on trays. Bake 5 minutes; cool on trays.
4 Spread half the florentine bases with white
chocolate; spread remaining bases with dark
chocolate. Run fork through chocolate to make
waves; stand at room temperature until set.
Store **florentines in an airtight container for up
to two weeks.**

frangipane jam drops

FRANGIPANE JAM DROPS

prep + cook time **45 minutes** makes **24**

125g butter, softened
½ teaspoon vanilla extract
½ cup (110g) caster sugar
1 cup (120g) ground almonds
1 egg
²/₃ cup (100g) plain flour
2 tablespoons raspberry jam

1 Preheat oven to 180°C/160°C fan forced.
Grease oven trays; line with baking paper.
2 Beat butter, extract, sugar and almond meal
in small bowl with electric mixer until light and
fluffy. Add egg, beating until just combined; stir
in sifted flour.
3 Drop level tablespoons of mixture on trays
5cm apart. Use handle of a wooden spoon to
make a small hole (about 1cm deep) in top of
each biscuit; fill each hole with ¼ teaspoon
jam. Bake about 15 minutes; cool jam drops
on trays.
Store **in an airtight container for up to a week.**

We used plain oval biscuits, spread with royal icing (see recipe on pg 72). Prepare decorations before spreading with icing, as the icing begins to set as soon as it is spread onto the biscuits. These biscuits are best eaten on the day they are iced.

ROCKET MAN

The two top sections are shaped from pieces taken from disassembled licorice allsorts; we used an M&M on the top section. The feet are made from fruit allsorts. Assemble the rocket man on the biscuit before the icing sets.

ABC

Letters like these pictured can be bought from confectionary shops or from supermarkets in the baking section. Or, cut letters from rolled-out ready-made soft icing or modelling paste. Position the lollies before the icing sets.

FAST BISCUITS

SPRINKLES

Coloured sprinkles and hundreds and thousands etc, come in all shapes, colours and sizes these days, and are usually found in the baking section of supermarkets. Sprinkle over the icing immediately before the icing sets.

RAINBOW STRIPES

Cut very fine strips from rainbow sour straps, then position the strips carefully on the icing before it sets.

We used plain oval biscuits, spread with royal icing (see recipe on pg 72). Prepare decorations before spreading with icing, as the icing begins to set as soon as it is spread onto the biscuits. These biscuits are best eaten on the day they are iced.

FUNNY FACES

Use Smarties or M&M's to make the eyes and noses; use rainbow choc chips to outline the mouths. Position lollies before the icing sets.

RIBBONS AND BOWS

We made the ribbons and bows by cutting very thin strips from red sour straps. Position the ribbons before the icing sets, secure the bows to the ribbons with a tiny dot of icing.

FAST BISCUITS

MINI MUSK DOTS

These little lollies come in various pastel shades, and are bought from confectionary shops. Push the lollies into the icing straight after the biscuits have been iced.

GHOSTS

These biscuits would be perfect for Halloween. Use fruit allsorts, sliced crossways for the eyes, and jelly beans for the mouths; position the lollies before the icing sets.

RASPBERRY COCONUT SLICE

prep + cook time 1 hour (+ cooling) **makes** 16

90g butter
½ cup (110g) caster sugar
1 egg
¼ cup (35g) self-raising flour
²/₃ cup (100g) plain flour
1 tablespoon custard powder
²/₃ cup (220g) raspberry jam
coconut topping
2 cups (160g) desiccated coconut
¼ cup (55g) caster sugar
2 eggs, beaten lightly

1 Preheat oven to 180°C/160°C fan-forced.
Grease 20cm x 30cm lamington pan; line base
and long sides with baking paper, extending
paper 5cm over sides.
2 Beat butter, sugar and egg in small bowl
with electric mixer until light and fluffy. Transfer
to medium bowl; stir in sifted flours and custard
powder. Spread dough into pan; spread
with jam.
3 Make coconut topping; sprinkle topping over
jam. Bake about 40 minutes; cool in pan before
cutting into pieces.
coconut topping Combine ingredients in
small bowl.
Store in an airtight container for up to a week.

SLICES

fig baklava

FIG BAKLAVA

prep + cook time **55 minutes (+ cooling)** makes **16**

1 cup (160g) roasted blanched almonds
1 cup (140g) roasted unsalted pistachios
1 cup (170g) coarsely chopped dried figs
2 teaspoons ground cinnamon
1 teaspoon ground cloves
1 teaspoon ground nutmeg
9 sheets fillo pastry
80g butter, melted
honey syrup
1 cup (250ml) water
¾ cup (165g) caster sugar
1/3 cup (115g) honey
1 teaspoon finely grated lemon rind

1 Preheat oven to 200°C/180°C fan-forced. Grease deep 22cm-square cake pan.
2 Blend or process nuts, figs and spices until chopped finely.
3 Cut pastry sheets in half crossways. Layer three pastry squares, brushing each sheet with butter; place in pan, sprinkle with ½ cup of the nut mixture. Repeat layering with remaining pastry, butter and nut mixture, ending with pastry.

4 Cut baklava into quarters; cut each quarter into four triangles. Bake 25 minutes.
5 Reduce oven temperature to 150°C/130°C fan-forced; bake baklava a further 10 minutes.
6 Meanwhile, make honey syrup.
7 Pour hot syrup over hot baklava; cool in pan.
honey syrup Combine ingredients in small saucepan. Stir over heat until sugar dissolves; bring to the boil. Reduce heat; simmer, uncovered, without stirring, 10 minutes.
Store in an airtight container for up to a week.

MUESLI SLICE

prep + cook time **40 minutes** makes **30**

125g butter, chopped coarsely
1/3 cup (75g) firmly packed brown sugar
2 tablespoons honey
11/3 cups (120g) rolled oats
½ cup (40g) shredded coconut
½ cup (75g) self-raising flour
½ cup (65g) dried cranberries
½ cup (80g) finely chopped dried pineapple
½ cup (70g) slivered almonds
2 tablespoons pepitas

1 Preheat oven to 180°C/160°C fan-forced. Grease 19cm x 30cm lamington pan; line base and long sides with baking paper, extending paper 5cm over sides.
2 Heat butter, sugar and honey in medium saucepan; stir until sugar dissolves. Stir in remaining ingredients.
3 Press mixture firmly into pan; bake about 20 minutes. Cool in pan before cutting.
Store in an airtight container for up to a week.

note Pepitas are also known as dried pumpkin seeds; they are available from health-food stores and most supermarkets.

muesli slice

VANILLA SLICE

prep + cook time **55 minutes (+ cooling and refrigeration)**
makes **16**

2 sheets ready-rolled puff pastry
½ cup (110g) caster sugar
½ cup (75g) cornflour
¼ cup (30g) custard powder
2½ cups (625ml) milk
30g butter
1 egg yolk
1 teaspoon vanilla extract
¾ cup (180ml) thickened cream
passionfruit icing
1½ cups (240g) icing sugar
1 teaspoon soft butter
¼ cup (60ml) passionfruit pulp (see note)

1 Preheat oven to 240°C/220°C fan-forced.
Grease deep 23cm-square cake pan; line with
foil, extending foil 10cm over sides of pan.
2 Place each pastry sheet on separate
greased oven trays. Bake about 15 minutes;
cool. Flatten pastry with hand; place one pastry
sheet in pan, trim to fit if necessary.
3 Meanwhile, combine sugar, cornflour and
custard powder in medium saucepan; gradually
add milk, stirring until smooth. Add butter;
stir over heat until mixture boils and thickens.
Simmer, stirring, about 3 minutes or until

custard is thick and smooth. Remove from
heat; stir in egg yolk and extract. Cover surface
of custard with plastic wrap; cool 10 minutes or
to room temperature.
4 Make passionfruit icing.
5 Whip cream until firm peaks form. Fold
cream into custard, in two batches. Spread
custard mixture over pastry in pan. Top with
remaining pastry, trim to fit if necessary; press
down slightly. Spread pastry with icing;
refrigerate 3 hours or overnight.
passionfruit icing Place sifted icing sugar,
butter and pulp in small heatproof bowl over
small saucepan of simmering water; stir until
icing is spreadable.
Store in an airtight container in the fridge for up to
three days.
note You need approximately three passionfruit for
this recipe.

triple choc brownies

TRIPLE CHOC BROWNIES

prep + cook time **1 hour** makes **16**

125g butter, chopped
200g dark eating chocolate, chopped
½ cup (110g) caster sugar
2 eggs
1¼ cups (185g) plain flour
150g white eating chocolate, chopped
100g milk eating chocolate, chopped

1 Preheat oven to 180°C/160°C fan-forced.
Grease deep 19cm-square cake pan; line base
and sides with baking paper, extending paper
5cm over sides.
2 Combine butter and dark chocolate in
medium saucepan; stir over low heat until
smooth. Cool 10 minutes.
3 Stir in sugar and eggs, then sifted flour and
white and milk chocolates. Spread mixture into
pan. Bake about 35 minutes. Cool in pan
before cutting.
Store in an airtight container, in the refrigerator, for
up to four days.

FRUIT MINCE SLICE

prep + cook time **1 hour (+ refrigeration)** makes **18**

¾ cup (110g) plain flour
½ cup (75g) self-raising flour
2 tablespoons caster sugar
100g cold butter, chopped coarsely
1 egg yolk
1 tablespoon milk
410g jar fruit mince
2 large apples (400g), peeled, grated coarsely
1 sheet puff pastry
1 egg yolk, extra

1 Grease 19cm x 30cm lamington pan; line
base and long sides with baking paper,
extending paper 5cm over sides.
2 Sift flours and sugar into large bowl; rub in
butter, then stir in egg yolk and milk. Turn
dough onto floured surface, knead gently until
smooth. Cover; refrigerate 30 minutes.
3 Preheat oven to 200°C/180°C fan-forced.
4 Roll dough between sheets of baking paper
until large enough to cover base of pan; press
into pan. Spread combined fruit mince and
apple over dough.
5 Cut pastry into 2cm-wide strips; place strips
over filling in a lattice pattern. Brush pastry with
a little extra egg yolk; bake slice about 30 minutes.
Cool in pan before cutting.
Store in an airtight container for up to four days.

fruit mince slice

chocolate caramel slice

CHOCOLATE CARAMEL SLICE

prep + cook time **45 minutes (+ refrigeration)** makes **16**

¾ cup (110g) plain flour
1/3 cup (25g) desiccated coconut
1/3 cup (75g) firmly packed brown sugar
90g butter, melted
395g can sweetened condensed milk
60g butter, extra
2 tablespoons maple syrup
200g dark eating chocolate,
    chopped coarsely
2 teaspoons vegetable oil

1 Preheat oven to 170°C/150°C fan-forced. Grease shallow 22cm-square cake pan; line base and sides with baking paper, extending paper 5cm above sides.
2 Combine sifted flour, coconut, sugar and butter in medium bowl; press mixture firmly over base of pan. Bake about 15 minutes or until browned lightly; cool slightly.
3 Meanwhile, combine condensed milk, extra butter and syrup in small saucepan; stir over medium heat until smooth, pour over base. Return to oven; bake 25 minutes. Cool.
4 Combine chocolate and oil in small saucepan; stir over low heat until smooth. Pour chocolate over caramel. Refrigerate slice about 3 hours or until set before cutting.
Store in an airtight container, in the refrigerator, for up to four days.

DATE SLICE

prep + cook time **1 hour 25 minutes (+ refrigeration)** makes **24**

1½ cups (225g) plain flour
1¼ cups (185g) self-raising flour
150g cold butter, chopped
1 tablespoon honey
1 egg
1/3 cup (80ml) milk, approximately
2 teaspoons milk, extra
1 tablespoon white sugar
date filling
3½ cups (500g) seeded dried dates,
    chopped coarsely

date slice

¾ cup (180ml) water
2 tablespoons finely grated lemon rind
2 tablespoons lemon juice

1 Grease 20cm x 30cm lamington pan; line base and long sides with baking paper, extending paper 5cm over sides.
2 Sift flours into large bowl; rub in butter until mixture is crumbly. Stir in combined honey and egg and enough milk to make a firm dough. Knead on floured surface until smooth, cover; refrigerate 30 minutes.
3 Meanwhile, make date filling.
4 Preheat oven to 200°C/180°C fan-forced.
5 Divide dough in half. Roll one half large enough to cover base of pan; press into pan, spread filling over dough. Roll remaining dough large enough to cover filling. Brush with extra milk; sprinkle with sugar. Bake about 20 minutes; cool in pan.
date filling Combine ingredients in medium saucepan; cook, stirring, about 10 minutes or until mixture is thick and smooth. Cool to room temperature.
Store in an airtight container for up to four days.

chewy chocolate slice

CHEWY CHOCOLATE SLICE

prep + cook time **50 minutes (+ cooling)** makes **12**

125g butter, melted
1 cup (220g) firmly packed brown sugar
1 egg, beaten lightly
1 teaspoon vanilla extract
½ cup (75g) plain flour
¼ cup (35g) self-raising flour
2 tablespoons cocoa powder
½ cup (45g) desiccated coconut
1 tablespoon desiccated coconut, extra
chocolate icing
1 cup (160g) icing sugar
2 tablespoons cocoa powder
10g butter, melted
1½ tablespoons hot water, approximately

1 Preheat oven to 180°C/160°C fan-forced.
Grease 19cm x 29cm rectangular slice pan;
line base and two long sides with baking paper,
extending paper 5cm above sides.
2 Combine butter, sugar, egg and extract in
medium bowl. Stir in sifted flours and cocoa
powder, then coconut.
3 Spread mixture evenly over base of pan.
Bake about 30 minutes or until firm.

4 Meanwhile, make chocolate icing.
5 Spread hot slice with chocolate icing; sprinkle
with extra coconut. Cool in pan before cutting.
chocolate icing Sift icing sugar and cocoa
into medium bowl; add combined butter and
water, stir until icing is a spreadable consistency.
Store in an airtight container for up to one week.

MIXED BERRY ALMOND AND COCONUT SLICE

prep + cook time **1 hour 25 minutes (+ cooling)**
makes **16**

2 cups (300g) frozen mixed berries
1 cup (220g) caster sugar
1 tablespoon lime juice
90g butter, softened
1 egg
²/₃ cup (100g) plain flour
¼ cup (35g) self-raising flour
1 tablespoon custard powder
almond coconut topping
2 eggs, beaten lightly
1½ cups (75g) flaked coconut
1 cup (80g) flaked almonds
¼ cup (55g) caster sugar

1 Preheat oven to 180°C/160°C fan-forced.
Grease 20cm x 30cm lamington pan; line base
and long sides with baking paper, extending
paper 5cm over sides.
2 Combine half the berries, half the sugar and
the juice in small saucepan; stir over low heat
until sugar dissolves. Bring to the boil; simmer,
uncovered, stirring occasionally, 20 minutes or
until mixture thickens; cool 10 minutes. Stir in
remaining berries.
3 Beat butter, egg and remaining sugar in bowl
with electric mixer until light and fluffy; stir in
sifted flours and custard powder. Spread
dough into pan; spread with berry mixture.
4 Make almond coconut topping; sprinkle over
berry mixture. Bake about 40 minutes; cool in
pan before cutting.
almond coconut topping Combine ingredients
in small bowl.
Store in an airtight container for up to a week.

mixed berry almond and coconut slice

APPLE PECAN STREUSEL MUFFINS

prep + cook time 1 hour (+ freezing) **makes** 12

4 medium apples (600g)
20g butter
$^1/_3$ cup (75g) firmly packed brown sugar
2 cups (300g) self-raising flour
¾ cup (165g) caster sugar
1 cup (120g) coarsely chopped
   roasted pecans
¾ cup (180ml) buttermilk
90g butter, melted
1 egg, beaten lightly
streusel topping
$^1/_3$ cup (50g) plain flour
2 tablespoons self-raising flour
¼ cup (55g) firmly packed brown sugar
½ teaspoon mixed spice
80g butter, chopped coarsely

1 Make streusel topping.
2 Preheat oven to 180°C/160°C fan-forced.
Grease two 6-hole ¾-cup (180ml) texas
muffin pans.
3 Peel, core and quarter apples; slice thinly.
Melt butter in large frying pan; cook apple,
stirring, about 5 minutes or until browned
lightly. Add brown sugar; cook, stirring, about
5 minutes or until mixture thickens slightly.
4 Sift flour into large bowl; stir in remaining
ingredients (do not over-mix; the batter should
be lumpy).
5 Spoon mixture into pan holes; top with apple
mixture. Coarsely grate streusel topping over
muffins; bake about 35 minutes. Stand muffins
in pans 5 minutes before turning, top-side up,
onto wire rack to cool.
streusel topping Process ingredients until
they come together. Enclose in plastic wrap;
freeze about 1 hour or until firm.
Store in an airtight container for up to four days.

CAKES &
LOAVES

scones

SCONES

prep + cook time **45 minutes** makes **20**

**4 cups (600g) self-raising flour
2 tablespoons icing sugar
60g butter
1½ cups (375ml) milk
¾ cup (180ml) water, approximately**

1 Preheat oven to 220°C/ 200°C fan-forced.
Grease 20cm x 30cm lamington pan.
2 Sift flour and icing sugar into large bowl;
rub in butter with fingertips.
3 Make a well in centre of flour mixture; add
milk and almost all the water. Use knife to cut
the milk and water through the flour mixture,
mixing to a soft, sticky dough. Knead dough
on floured surface until smooth.
4 Press dough out to 2cm thickness. Dip
4.5cm round cutter in flour; cut as many rounds
as you can from dough. Place scones, side by
side, just touching, in pan.
5 Gently knead scraps of dough together;
repeat pressing and cutting of dough, place in
pan. Brush tops with a little extra milk; bake
about 15 minutes or until scones are just
browned and sound hollow when tapped
firmly on the top with fingers.

Scones are best made and eaten on the same day. Or,
freeze for up to 3 months; thaw in oven, wrapped in foil.

berry buttermilk muffins

BERRY BUTTERMILK MUFFINS

prep + cook time **30 minutes** makes **12**

**2½ cups (375g) self-raising flour
100g butter, chopped coarsely
1 cup (220g) caster sugar
1¼ cups (310ml) buttermilk
1 egg, beaten lightly
1⅓ cups (200g) frozen mixed berries**

1 Preheat oven to 200°C/180°C fan-forced.
Line 12-hole (⅓-cup/80ml) muffin pan with
paper cases.
2 Sift flour into large bowl; rub in butter with
fingertips. Stir in sugar, buttermilk and egg.
Do not over-mix; mixture should be lumpy.
Stir in berries.
3 Divide mixture among pan holes. Bake
about 20 minutes. Stand muffins in pan
5 minutes before turning, top-side up, onto
wire rack to cool.

Store in an airtight container for up to two days.
note Use any type of frozen or fresh berries.

variation
mango buttermilk muffins Omit the raspberries and
replace with 1 small finely chopped fresh mango (300g).

carrot cupcakes with maple frosting

CARROT CUPCAKES WITH MAPLE FROSTING

prep + cook time **1 hour** makes **12**

½ cup (125ml) vegetable oil
3 eggs
1½ cups (225g) self-raising flour
1 cup (220g) firmly packed brown sugar
2 teaspoons mixed spice
2 cups (480g) firmly packed coarsely grated carrot (see note)
¾ cup (90g) coarsely chopped roasted pecans
6 roasted whole pecans, halved
maple frosting
30g butter, softened
80g cream cheese, softened
2 tablespoons maple syrup
1¼ cups (200g) icing sugar

1 Preheat oven to 180°C/160°C fan-forced. Line 12-hole (⅓-cup/80ml) muffin pan with paper cases.
2 Stir oil, eggs, sifted flour, sugar and spice in medium bowl until combined. Stir in carrot and chopped nuts.
3 Divide mixture among paper cases; bake about 30 minutes. Stand cupcakes in pan 5 minutes before turning, top-side up, onto wire rack to cool.
4 Meanwhile, make maple frosting. Spread frosting over cupcakes; top each with a nut.
maple frosting Beat butter, cream cheese and syrup in small bowl with electric mixer until light and fluffy; gradually beat in sifted icing sugar until frosting is spreadable.
Store iced cakes in an airtight container, in the refrigerator, for up to two days.
note You need four medium carrots for this recipe.

LAMINGTONS

prep + cook time **1 hour** makes **16**

6 eggs
⅔ cup (150g) caster sugar
⅓ cup (50g) cornflour
½ cup (75g) plain flour
⅓ cup (50g) self-raising flour
2 cups (160g) desiccated coconut
chocolate icing
4 cups (640g) icing sugar
½ cup (50g) cocoa powder
15g butter, melted
1 cup (250ml) milk

1 Preheat oven to 180°C/160°C fan-forced. Grease 20cm x 30cm lamington pan; line base and long sides with baking paper, extending paper 5cm over sides.
2 Beat eggs in large bowl with electric mixer about 10 minutes or until thick and creamy; gradually beat in sugar, dissolving between additions. Fold in triple-sifted flours.
3 Spread mixture into pan; bake about 35 minutes. Turn cake immediately onto a baking-paper-covered wire rack to cool.
4 Meanwhile, make chocolate icing. Cut cake into 16 squares; dip each square in icing, drain off excess. Toss squares in coconut. Place lamingtons onto wire rack to set.
chocolate icing Sift icing sugar and cocoa into medium heatproof bowl; stir in butter and milk. Set bowl over medium saucepan of simmering water; stir until icing is of a coating consistency.
Store lamingtons in an airtight container for up to three days.

lamingtons

PATTY CAKES WITH GLACÉ ICING

prep + cook time **45 minutes** makes **12**

125g butter, softened
½ teaspoon vanilla extract
¾ cup (165g) caster sugar
3 eggs
2 cups (300g) self-raising flour
¼ cup (60ml) milk
glacé icing
2 cups (320g) icing sugar
20g butter, melted
2 tablespoons hot water, approximately

1 Preheat oven to 180°C/160°C fan-forced. Line 12-hole (⅓-cup/80ml) muffin pan with paper cases.
2 Place ingredients in medium bowl; beat with electric mixer on low speed until ingredients are combined. Increase speed to medium; beat about 3 minutes or until mixture is smooth and paler in colour.

3 Divide mixture among paper cases. Bake about 25 minutes. Stand cakes in pan 5 minutes before turning, top-side up, onto wire racks to cool.
4 Meanwhile, make glacé icing. Spread cool cakes with icing.
glacé icing Sift icing sugar into small heatproof bowl; stir in butter and enough of the water to make a firm paste. Stir over small saucepan of simmering water until icing is spreadable.

Store iced cakes in an airtight container, in the refrigerator, for up to two days.

cake variations
berry & orange Stir in 1 teaspoon finely grated orange rind and ½ cup dried mixed berries at the end of step 2.
citrus Stir in ½ teaspoon each of finely grated lime, orange and lemon rind at the end of step 2.
passionfruit & white chocolate Stir in ¼ cup passionfruit pulp and ½ cup white Choc Bits at the end of step 2.

icing variations
coconut & lime Stir in ½ teaspoon coconut essence and 1 teaspoon finely grated lime rind.
orange Stir in 1 teaspoon finely grated orange rind. Replace 1 tablespoon of the hot water with orange juice.

MARBLE CAKE

prep + cook time **1 hour 30 minutes** serves **12**

1 quantity basic buttercake mixture
  (see recipe, opposite)
pink food colouring
2 tablespoons cocoa powder
2 tablespoons milk, extra
butter frosting
90g butter, softened
1 cup (160g) icing sugar
1 tablespoon milk

1 Follow steps 1 and 2 in basic buttercake recipe, opposite.
2 Divide mixture among three bowls; tint one mixture pink. Blend sifted cocoa with extra milk in cup; stir into second mixture, leave remaining mixture plain.
3 Drop alternate spoonfuls of all mixtures into pan. Pull a skewer backwards and forwards through cake mixture.
4 Bake cake about 1 hour. Stand cake in pan 5 minutes before turning, top-side up, onto wire rack to cool.
5 Make butter frosting; top cake with frosting.
butter frosting Beat butter in small bowl with electric mixer until light and fluffy; beat in sifted icing sugar and milk, in two batches. Tint frosting pink with colouring.

Store in an airtight container for up to two days.

basic buttercake

BASIC BUTTERCAKE

prep + cook time **1 hour 30 minutes** serves **12**

250g butter, softened
1 teaspoon vanilla extract
1¼ cups (275g) caster sugar
3 eggs
2¼ cups (335g) self-raising flour
¾ cup (180ml) milk

1 Preheat oven to 180°C/160°C fan-forced. Grease deep 22cm-round or 19cm-square cake pan; line with baking paper.
2 Beat butter, extract and sugar in medium bowl with electric mixer until light and fluffy. Beat in eggs, one at a time. Stir in sifted flour and milk, in two batches.
3 Spread mixture into pan; bake about 1 hour. Stand cake in pan 5 minutes before turning, top-side up, onto wire rack to cool.

Store in an airtight container for up to two days.

marble cake

rhubarb custard tea cake

RHUBARB CUSTARD TEA CAKE

prep + cook time **1 hour 50 minutes (+ cooling)** serves **8**

200g butter, softened
½ cup (110g) caster sugar
2 eggs
1¼ cups (185g) self-raising flour
$^{1}/_{3}$ cup (40g) custard powder
4 fresh rhubarb stalks (300g), sliced
    lengthways then cut into 10cm lengths
20g butter, melted
2 teaspoons caster sugar, extra
custard
2 tablespoons custard powder
¼ cup (55g) caster sugar
1 cup (250ml) milk
20g butter
2 teaspoons vanilla extract

1 Make custard.
2 Preheat oven to 180°C/160°C fan-forced.
Grease deep 20cm-round cake pan; line base
with baking paper.
3 Beat softened butter and sugar in small bowl
with electric mixer until light and fluffy. Beat in
eggs, one at a time. Transfer to medium bowl;
stir in sifted flour and custard powder.
4 Spread half the mixture into pan; spread over
custard. Dollop small spoonfuls of remaining
cake mixture over custard; carefully spread
with spatula to completely cover custard. Top
cake mixture with rhubarb; brush gently with
melted butter then sprinkle with extra sugar.
5 Bake cake about 1¼ hours; cool in pan.
custard Combine custard powder and sugar
in small saucepan; gradually stir in milk. Cook,
stirring, until mixture boils and thickens slightly.
Remove from heat; stir in butter and extract.
Press plastic wrap over surface of custard to
prevent a skin forming; cool. Whisk until
smooth before using.
Store cake in the freezer for up to two months. Cake
is best eaten on day it is made.

sponge cake

SPONGE CAKE

prep + cook time **40 minutes** serves **10**

4 eggs
¾ cup (165g) caster sugar
$^{2}/_{3}$ cup (100g) wheaten cornflour
¼ cup (30g) custard powder
1 teaspoon cream of tartar
½ teaspoon bicarbonate of soda
$^{1}/_{3}$ cup (110g) apricot jam
300ml thickened cream, whipped

1 Preheat oven to 180°C/160°C fan-forced.
Grease and flour two deep 22cm-round
cake pans.
2 Beat eggs and sugar in small bowl with
electric mixer until thick and creamy and sugar
is dissolved; transfer to large bowl.
3 Fold in triple-sifted dry ingredients. Divide
mixture between pans; bake about 20 minutes.
Turn sponges, top-side up, onto baking-paper-
lined wire rack to cool.
4 Sandwich sponges with jam and cream.
Store unfilled sponge in the freezer for up to two months.
Filled sponge is best eaten on day it is made.

caramel mud cake

CARAMEL MUD CAKE

prep + cook time **2 hours (+ cooling)** serves **12**

180g white eating chocolate, chopped
185g unsalted butter, chopped
1 cup (220g) firmly packed brown sugar
¹/₃ cup (80ml) golden syrup
1 cup (250ml) milk
1½ cups (225g) plain flour
½ cup (75g) self-raising flour
2 eggs
white chocolate ganache
½ cup (125ml) cream
360g white eating chocolate, chopped

1 Preheat oven to 160°C/140°C fan-forced.
Grease deep 22cm-round cake pan; line with
baking paper.
2 Combine chocolate, butter, sugar, syrup and
milk in large saucepan; stir over low heat until
smooth. Cool 15 minutes.
3 Whisk in sifted flours and eggs. Pour mixture
into pan; bake about 1½ hours. Cool cake in pan.
4 Meanwhile, make white chocolate ganache.
5 Turn cake, top-side up, onto plate; spread
with ganache.

white chocolate ganache Bring cream to
the boil in small saucepan, remove from heat;
add chocolate, stir until smooth. Refrigerate,
stirring occasionally, about 30 minutes or until
ganache is spreadable.
Store in an airtight container, in the refrigerator, for up
to a week, or freeze for up to two months.

WHITE MUD CAKE

prep + cook time **2½ hours (+ cooling)** serves **12**

180g white chocolate, chopped
350g unsalted butter, chopped
2²/₃ cups (590g) caster sugar
1½ cups (375ml) milk
2 cups (300g) plain flour
²/₃ cup (100g) self-raising flour
1 teaspoon vanilla extract
3 eggs
white chocolate ganache
½ cup (125ml) cream
360g white eating chocolate, chopped

1 Preheat oven to 160°C/140°C fan-forced.
Grease deep 22cm-round cake pan; line with
baking paper.
2 Combine chocolate, butter, sugar and milk in
large saucepan; stir over low heat until smooth.
Pour mixture into large bowl; cool 15 minutes.
3 Whisk in sifted flours, extract and eggs. Pour
mixture into pan; bake about 2 hours. Cool
cake in pan.
4 Meanwhile, make white chocolate ganache.
5 Turn cake, top-side up, onto plate; spread
with ganache.

white chocolate ganache Bring cream to
the boil in small saucepan, remove from heat;
add chocolate, stir until smooth. Refrigerate,
stirring occasionally, about 30 minutes or until
ganache is spreadable.
Store in an airtight container, in the refrigerator, for up
to a week, or freeze for up to two months.

banana cake with passionfruit icing

BANANA CAKE WITH PASSIONFRUIT ICING

prep + cook time **1 hour 15 minutes** serves **10**

160g butter, softened
¾ cup (165g) firmly packed brown sugar
2 eggs
1½ cups (350g) mashed banana (see note)
1 teaspoon bicarbonate of soda
2 tablespoons hot milk
1 cup (150g) plain flour
²/₃ cup (100g) self-raising flour
passionfruit icing
1 cup (160g) icing sugar
2 tablespoons passionfruit pulp,
    approximately

1 Preheat oven to 180°C/160°C. Grease deep 20cm-round cake pan; line base and side with baking paper.
2 Beat butter and sugar in small bowl with electric mixer until light and fluffy. Beat in eggs, one at a time. Transfer mixture to large bowl; stir in banana. Combine soda and milk in small jug; stir into banana mixture. Stir in sifted flours in two batches. Spread mixture into pan.
3 Bake about 45 minutes. Stand cake in pan 5 minutes before turning, top-side up, onto wire rack to cool.
4 Meanwhile, make passionfruit icing. Drizzle cake with icing.
passionfruit icing Sift icing sugar into small bowl; stir in enough of the passionfruit pulp until icing is pourable.
Store in an airtight container for up to four days.
note You need 3 large overripe bananas (690g) to get the amount of mashed banana needed for this recipe.

DARK CHOCOLATE MUD CAKE

prep + cook time **2 hours (+ cooling)** serves **12**

250g unsalted butter, chopped
2 cups (440g) caster sugar
½ cup (125ml) milk
½ cup (125ml) strong black coffee
½ cup (125ml) bourbon
1 teaspoon vanilla extract
200g dark eating chocolate, chopped coarsely
1½ cups (225g) plain flour

dark chocolate mud cake

¼ cup (35g) self-raising flour
¼ cup (25g) cocoa powder
2 eggs
dark chocolate ganache
½ cup (125ml) cream
200g dark eating chocolate, chopped coarsely

1 Preheat oven to 160°C/140°C fan-forced. Grease deep 23cm-square cake pan; line base with baking paper.
2 Combine butter, sugar, milk, coffee, bourbon, extract and chocolate in medium saucepan; stir over low heat until smooth. Transfer to large bowl; cool 15 minutes. Whisk in sifted flours and cocoa, then eggs.
3 Pour mixture into pan; bake about 1½ hours.
4 Stand cake in pan 5 minutes before turning, top-side up, onto wire rack to cool.
5 Meanwhile, make dark chocolate ganache. Spread cold cake with ganache.
dark chocolate ganache Bring cream to the boil in small saucepan. Remove from heat, add chocolate; stir until smooth. Stand 10 minutes before using.
Store in an airtight container, in the refrigerator, for up to a week, or freeze for up to two months.

BLACK FOREST CAKE

prep + cook time **2 hours 25 minutes** (+ cooling)
serves **12**

250g butter, chopped
1 tablespoon instant coffee granules
1½ cups (375ml) hot water
200g dark eating chocolate, chopped
2 cups (440g) caster sugar
1½ cups (225g) self-raising flour
1 cup (150g) plain flour
¼ cup (25g) cocoa powder
2 eggs
2 teaspoons vanilla extract
¼ cup (60ml) kirsch
600ml thickened cream, whipped
2 x 425g cans seeded black cherries,
    drained, halved
2 teaspoons cocoa powder, extra

1 Preheat oven to 150°C/130°C fan-forced.
Grease deep 22cm-round cake pan, line base
and side with baking paper.
2 Melt butter in medium saucepan; stir in
combined coffee and hot water, then chocolate
and sugar. Stir over low heat, without boiling,
until smooth. Transfer mixture to large bowl,
cool slightly.
3 Beat chocolate mixture on low speed with
electric mixer; gradually beat in sifted dry
ingredients, in three batches. Beat in eggs,
one at a time, then extract.
4 Pour mixture into pan; bake about 1¾ hours.
Stand cake in pan 5 minutes before turning,
top-side up, onto wire rack to cool.
5 Trim top of cold cake to make flat. Split cake
into three equal layers. Place one layer onto
serving plate; brush with half the kirsch, top
with half the cream and half the cherries.
Repeat layering, then top with cake top. Dust
with extra sifted cocoa.

Store unfilled cakes in an airtight container for up to
two days. Filled cake can be refrigerated in an airtight
container for to up two days.

cinnamon tea cake

CINNAMON TEA CAKE

prep + cook time **50 minutes** serves **10**

60g butter, softened
1 teaspoon vanilla extract
²/₃ cup (150g) caster sugar
1 egg
1 cup (150g) self-raising flour
¹/₃ cup (80ml) milk
10g butter, extra, melted
1 teaspoon ground cinnamon
1 tablespoon caster sugar, extra

1 Preheat oven to 180°C/160°C fan-forced. Grease deep 20cm-round cake pan; line base with baking paper.
2 Beat butter, extract, sugar and egg in small bowl with electric mixer until light and fluffy. Stir in sifted flour and milk.
3 Spread mixture into pan; bake about 30 minutes. Stand cake in pan 5 minutes before turning, top-side up, onto wire rack. Brush top of cake with melted butter; sprinkle with combined cinnamon and extra sugar.
4 Serve warm with whipped cream or butter.
Tea cake is best eaten on the day it is made.

COCONUT CAKE

prep + cook time **1 hour** serves **20**

125g butter, softened
½ teaspoon coconut essence
1 cup (220g) caster sugar
2 eggs
½ cup (40g) desiccated coconut
1½ cups (225g) self-raising flour
1¼ cups (300g) sour cream
¹/₃ cup (80ml) milk
coconut ice frosting
2 cups (320g) icing sugar
1¹/₃ cups (100g) desiccated coconut
2 egg whites, beaten lightly
pink food colouring

1 Preheat oven to 180°C/160°C fan-forced. Grease deep 23cm-square cake pan; line with baking paper.

coconut cake

2 Beat butter, essence and sugar in small bowl with electric mixer until light and fluffy. Beat in eggs, one at a time. Transfer mixture to large bowl; stir in coconut, sifted flour, sour cream and milk, in two batches.
3 Spread mixture into pan; bake about 40 minutes. Stand cake in pan 5 minutes before turning, top-side up, onto wire rack to cool.
4 Meanwhile, make coconut ice frosting. Drop alternate spoonfuls of white and pink frosting onto cake; marble over top of cake.
coconut ice frosting Sift icing sugar into medium bowl; stir in coconut and egg white. Place half the mixture in small bowl; tint with pink colouring.
Store in an airtight container for up to a week.

divine ginger cake

DIVINE GINGER CAKE

prep + cook time 1 hour 5 minutes serves 10

¾ cup (165g) firmly packed brown sugar
¾ cup (110g) plain flour
½ cup (75g) self-raising flour
½ teaspoon bicarbonate of soda
2 teaspoons ground ginger
1 teaspoon ground cinnamon
½ teaspoon ground nutmeg
125g butter, softened
2 eggs
²/₃ cup (160ml) buttermilk
caramel icing
60g butter
½ cup (110g) firmly packed brown sugar
2 tablespoons milk
¾ cup (120g) icing sugar

1 Preheat oven to 170°C/150°C fan-forced.
Grease deep 20cm ring pan.
2 Sift dry ingredients into medium bowl. Add
remaining ingredients; beat with electric mixer
on low speed until ingredients are combined.
Increase speed to medium; beat 2 minutes or
until mixture is smooth and paler in colour.

3 Pour mixture into pan; bake cake about
35 minutes. Stand cake in pan 10 minutes
before turning, top-side up, onto wire rack
to cool.
4 Meanwhile, make caramel icing. Drizzle
warm icing over cake.
caramel icing Stir butter, brown sugar and
milk in small saucepan over heat until sugar
dissolves. Bring to the boil, then simmer,
stirring, 2 minutes. Remove from heat, stir
in sifted icing sugar.
Store in an airtight container for up to a week.
note This cake will almost certainly crack, as
most ring-shaped cakes do; however, the icing
will cover them.

SPONGE ROLL WITH JAM AND CREAM

prep + cook time 40 minutes (+ refrigeration) serves 10

3 eggs
²/₃ cup (150g) caster sugar
½ cup (75g) wheaten cornflour
2 tablespoons custard powder
¾ teaspoon cream of tartar
½ teaspoon bicarbonate of soda
¹/₃ cup (110g) raspberry jam
¾ cup (180ml) thickened cream, whipped

1 Preheat oven to 180°C/160°C fan-forced.
Grease 25cm x 30cm swiss roll pan; line base
with baking paper, extending paper 5cm over
long sides.
2 Beat eggs and ½ cup of the caster sugar in
small bowl with electric mixer until thick and
creamy and sugar is dissolved.
3 Fold in triple-sifted dry ingredients. Spread
mixture into pan; bake about 12 minutes.
4 Meanwhile, place a piece of baking paper
cut the same size as the pan on bench;
sprinkle with remaining caster sugar. Turn
sponge onto paper; peel lining paper away.
Cool; trim all sides of sponge.
5 Spread sponge with jam then cream. Using
paper as a guide, roll sponge from short side.
Cover with plastic wrap; refrigerate 30 minutes.
Sponge roll is best eaten on the day it is made.

sponge roll with jam and cream

cherry and sultana buttercake

CHERRY AND SULTANA BUTTERCAKE

prep + cook time **1 hour 30 minutes** serves **12**

250g butter, softened
1 teaspoon vanilla extract
1 cup (220g) caster sugar
3 eggs
1¼ cups (185g) plain flour
1 cup (150g) self-raising flour
⅓ cup (80ml) milk
1 cup (160g) sultanas
¾ cup (150g) coarsely chopped
   red glacé cherries
coconut frosting
1 cup (160g) icing sugar
¾ cup (60g) desiccated coconut
1 egg white
pink food colouring

1 Preheat oven to 180°C/160°C fan-forced. Grease deep 22cm-round cake pan; line with baking paper.
2 Beat butter, extract and sugar in medium bowl with electric mixer until light and fluffy. Beat in eggs, one at a time. Stir in sifted flours and milk, in two batches. Stir in sultanas and cherries.
3 Spread mixture into pan; bake about 1 hour. Stand cake in pan 5 minutes before turning, top-side up, onto wire rack to cool.
4 Meanwhile, make coconut frosting. Top cake with coconut frosting.
coconut frosting Sift icing sugar into medium bowl; stir in coconut and egg white until combined; tint lightly with pink colouring.
Store cake in an airtight container for up to two days; un-iced cake can be frozen for up to two months.

MADEIRA CAKE

prep + cook time **1 hour 15 minutes** serves **12**

180g butter, softened
2 teaspoons finely grated lemon rind
⅔ cup (150g) caster sugar
3 eggs
¾ cup (110g) plain flour
¾ cup (110g) self-raising flour

madeira cake

⅓ cup (55g) mixed peel
¼ cup (35g) slivered almonds

1 Preheat oven to 160°C/140°C fan-forced. Grease deep 20cm-round cake pan; line base with paper.
2 Beat butter, rind and sugar in small bowl with electric mixer until light and fluffy; beat in eggs, one at a time. Transfer mixture to large bowl, stir in sifted flours.
3 Spread mixture into pan; bake 20 minutes. Remove cake from oven; sprinkle with peel and nuts. Return to oven; bake about 40 minutes. Stand cake in pan 5 minutes before turning, top-side up, onto wire rack to cool.
Store madeira cake in an airtight container for up to four days.

DATE AND PECAN ROLL

prep + cook time **1 hour 15 minutes** serves **10**

30g butter
½ cup (125ml) boiling water
½ cup (90g) finely chopped dried
    seeded dates
¼ teaspoon bicarbonate of soda
½ cup (110g) firmly packed brown sugar
1 cup (150g) self-raising flour
¼ cup (30g) coarsely chopped pecans
1 egg

1 Adjust oven shelves to fit upright nut roll tins. Preheat oven to 170°C/150°C fan-forced. Grease lids and inside of 8cm x 20cm nut roll tin evenly with melted butter; place base lid on tin, position tin upright on oven tray.
2 Stir butter and the water in medium saucepan over low heat until butter melts. Remove from heat; stir in dates and soda, then remaining ingredients. Spoon mixture into tin; tap tin firmly on bench to remove air pockets; position top lid.
3 Bake roll about 1 hour. Stand roll in tin 5 minutes; remove lids. Shake tin gently to release roll onto wire rack. Serve sliced, warm or cold, with butter.

Store in an airtight container for up to three days. Nut rolls can be frozen for up to two months.

tip Tall 850ml (8cm x 17cm) fruit juice cans make good nut roll tins. Use a can opener that cuts just below the rims to cut one end from the can. Wash and dry the can thoroughly before greasing. Use a double-thickness of foil to cover top of the can and secure with string; slash a hole in the foil top to allow steam to escape during baking.
The tin needs to be coated thickly with melted butter so the roll won't stick to the inside of the tin. Don't use cooking-oil spray, as this doesn't give a good enough coating and the roll will stick and be hard to turn out.

chocolate cake

CHOCOLATE CAKE

prep + cook time **1 hour 10 minutes** serves **20**

125g butter, softened
1 teaspoon vanilla extract
1¼ cups (275g) caster sugar
2 eggs
1¹/₃ cups (200g) self-raising flour
½ cup (50g) cocoa powder
²/₃ cup cup (160ml) water
chocolate icing
90g dark eating chocolate, chopped coarsely
30g butter
1 cup (160g) icing sugar
2 tablespoons hot water

1 Preheat oven to 180°C/160°C fan-forced.
Grease deep 20cm-round cake pan; line with
baking paper.
2 Beat ingredients in large bowl with electric
mixer on low speed until ingredients are
combined. Increase speed to medium; beat
about 3 minutes or until mixture is smooth and
paler in colour.
3 Spread mixture into pan; bake about 1 hour.
Stand cake in pan 5 minutes before turning,
top-side up, onto wire rack to cool.
4 Meanwhile, make chocolate icing. Spread
cake with icing.
chocolate icing Melt chocolate and butter
in small heatproof bowl over small saucepan
of simmering water; gradually stir in sifted
icing sugar and the hot water, stirring until
icing is spreadable.
Store **chocolate cake in an airtight container for
up to three days.**

BANANA BREAD

prep + cook time **1 hour 20 minutes** serves **12**

1 cup mashed banana (see note)
1 cup (220g) firmly packed dark brown sugar
2 eggs, beaten lightly
40g butter, melted
½ cup (125ml) buttermilk
¼ cup (90g) treacle
1½ cups (225g) plain flour
1 cup (150g) self-raising flour

banana bread

2 teaspoons mixed spice
1 teaspoon bicarbonate of soda

1 Preheat oven to 180°C/160°C fan-forced.
Grease 14cm x 21cm loaf pan; line base and
long sides with baking paper, extending paper
5cm over sides.
2 Combine banana, sugar, egg, butter,
buttermilk and treacle in large bowl; stir in sifted
dry ingredients (do not over-mix; the batter
should be lumpy). Spoon mixture into pan.
3 Bake about 1 hour. Stand bread in pan
10 minutes before turning, top-side up, onto
wire rack to cool.
Store **in an airtight container for up to a week.**

notes You need two large overripe bananas (460g) to
get the amount of mashed banana needed for this
recipe. For an authentic café experience, lightly toast
the banana bread and serve it with butter.

mini sultana loaves

lemon glacé icing Sift icing sugar into small heatproof bowl; stir in butter and enough juice to make a firm paste. Stir over small saucepan of simmering water until icing is pourable.
Store in an airtight container for up to three days.

POLENTA AND ALMOND ORANGE CAKE

prep + cook time 3¼ hours serves 12

2 medium oranges (480g)
⅔ cup (110g) roasted blanched almonds
¾ cup (165g) caster sugar
1 teaspoon baking powder
6 eggs
1 cup (120g) ground almonds
1 cup (170g) polenta
50g butter, melted

1 Cover unpeeled whole oranges in medium saucepan with cold water, bring to the boil. Boil, uncovered, 30 minutes; drain. Repeat process with fresh water, boil about 1 hour or until oranges are tender; drain. Cool oranges.
2 Preheat oven to 200°C/180°C fan-forced. Grease deep 22cm-round cake pan; line base and side with baking paper.
3 Blend or process nuts with 1 tablespoon of the sugar until coarse.
4 Trim ends from oranges then cut in half; discard seeds. Blend or process oranges, including rind, with baking powder until mixture is pulpy.
5 Beat eggs with remaining sugar in small bowl with electric mixer until light and fluffy. Transfer to large bowl; fold in nut mixture, ground almonds, polenta, butter and orange pulp.
6 Spread mixture into pan; bake about 50 minutes. Cool cake in pan 5 minutes before turning cake, top-side up, onto serving plate; serve dusted with sifted icing sugar, if you like.
Store in an airtight container, in the refrigerator, for up to three days.

MINI SULTANA LOAVES

prep + cook time 55 minutes makes 8

125g butter, melted
2⅓ cups (375g) sultanas
⅔ cup (150g) caster sugar
2 eggs
⅓ cup (80ml) buttermilk
½ cup (75g) plain flour
¾ cup (110g) self-raising flour
lemon glacé icing
1½ cups (240g) icing sugar
20g softened butter
2 tablespoons lemon juice, approximately

1 Preheat oven to 160°C/140°C fan-forced. Grease 8-hole (¾-cup/180ml) petite loaf pan.
2 Stir ingredients in large bowl with wooden spoon until combined.
3 Divide mixture into pan holes, smooth tops; bake about 30 minutes. Stand cakes in pan 5 minutes before turning, top-side up, onto wire rack to cool.
4 Meanwhile, make lemon glacé icing. Drizzle icing over cakes.

polenta and almond orange cake

ECONOMICAL BOILED FRUIT CAKE

prep + cook time **1 hour 45 minutes (+ cooling)**
serves **12**

2¾ cups (500g) mixed dried fruit
½ cup (125ml) water
1 cup (220g) firmly packed brown sugar
125g butter, chopped
1 teaspoon mixed spice
½ teaspoon bicarbonate of soda
½ cup (125ml) sweet sherry
1 egg
1 cup (150g) plain flour
1 cup (150g) self-raising flour
⅓ cup (55g) blanched almonds
2 tablespoons sweet sherry, extra

1 Combine fruit, the water, sugar, butter, spice and soda in large saucepan. Stir over low heat, without boiling, until sugar dissolves and butter melts; bring to the boil. Reduce heat; simmer, covered, 5 minutes. Remove from heat; stir in sherry. Cool to room temperature.

2 Preheat oven to 160°C/140°C fan-forced. Grease deep 20cm-round cake pan; line base and side with two layers of baking paper, extending paper 5cm above side.

3 Stir egg and sifted flours into fruit mixture. Spread mixture into pan; decorate with nuts. Bake about 1½ hours. Brush top of hot cake with extra sherry. Cover cake with foil, cool in pan.

Store fruit cake in an airtight container for up to one month.

Decorate any of your favourite cupcakes with these simple ideas. See pg 72 for frosting and icing recipes. Cakes are best eaten on the day they are iced.

FRUITY STRIPES

Make butter cream; spread over cake tops. Halve yellow and orange fruit sticks crossways. Trim ends of the fruit sticks to fit neatly on the top of each cake.

SPIRALS

Make butter cream; colour with lemon/yellow food colouring. Spread cake tops with the butter cream. Make spirals, starting from the centre of the cake, using different sized yellow lollies – we used rainbow chips, then mini M&M's and Smarties to create the spiral.

CELEBRATION CUPCAKES

WHITE CHOC CURLS

Make white chocolate ganache. Use a sharp vegetable peeler to make chocolate curls by shaving the curls from the side of a bar of white chocolate. Spread top of each cake generously with ganache; top with the chocolate curls.

TOASTY COCONUT

Make cream cheese frosting. Stir coarsely flaked coconut in a frying pan over a low heat until it is browned lightly; remove from the pan immediately to cool. Spread the top of each cake generously with frosting; sprinkle with the toasted coconut.

Decorate any of your favourite cupcakes with these simple ideas. See pg 72 for frosting and icing recipes. Cakes are best eaten on the day they are iced.

MINTY SNOWFLAKES

Make butter cream; colour with blue food colouring. Spread cake tops evenly with butter cream. Gently push mini mints into butter cream in the shape of snowflakes. Dust cakes with sifted icing sugar.

CHRISTMAS WREATHS

Make butter cream; colour with white food colouring. Spread cake tops with a thick layer of butter cream. Split spearmint leaf lollies in half horizontally (you'll need about six leaves for each cake). Gently push leaves, smooth-side up and slightly overlapping, into butter cream in the shape of a wreath. Decorate leaves with silver and gold cachous.

CELEBRATION CUPCAKES

RAINBOWS

Make dark chocolate ganache. Fit a large piping bag with a large fluted tube, half-fill the bag with ganache. Pipe generous swirls on the top of each cake. Decorate cakes with multi-coloured Smarties and rainbow chips.

PEANUT HEAVEN

Make milk chocolate ganache; marble some chunky peanut butter through ganache. Fit a large piping bag with a large fluted tube, half-fill the bag with ganache. Pipe generous swirls of ganache on top of each cake; sprinkle with crushed peanut brittle.

BUTTER CREAM

makes 1¾ cups

Beat 125g softened butter in small bowl with electric mixer until as white as possible; beat in 1½ cups sifted icing sugar and 2 tablespoons milk, in two batches.

tips Add any flavoured essence or extract you like to the butter cream. Beat it with the butter for the best flavour. Any citrus rind can be added. Beat 2 teaspoons finely grated rind with the butter and use the corresponding juice instead of the milk.
Butter cream is the most popular type of frosting, it's easy to spread and handle. Be aware that it's cream in colour, so any added colouring will result in the final colour being slightly yellow, particularly pinks and reds.

FLUFFY FROSTING

makes 2½ cups

Combine 1 cup caster sugar and ¹⁄₃ cup water in small saucepan; stir over heat, without boiling, until sugar is dissolved. Boil, uncovered, without stirring, about 5 minutes or until syrup reaches 116°C on a candy thermometer. Syrup should be thick but not coloured. Remove from heat, allow bubbles to subside. Beat 2 egg whites in small bowl with electric mixer until soft peaks form. While motor is operating, add hot syrup in a thin stream; beat on high speed about 10 minutes or until mixture is thick.

tip If you don't have a candy thermometer, boil the syrup until it's thick with heavy bubbles, but not coloured. Remove from heat, let bubbles subside, then reassess the thickness of the syrup.

ROYAL ICING

makes 1 cup

Sift 1½ cups icing sugar through a very fine sieve. Lightly beat 1 egg white in small bowl with an electric mixer; add icing sugar, one tablespoon at a time. When icing reaches firm peaks, use a wooden spoon to beat in ½ teaspoon lemon juice; cover tightly with plastic wrap.

tip Royal icing begins to set as soon as it's exposed to the air, so keep the icing covered tightly with plastic wrap while you're not working with it. Stir in a few drops of food colouring if required by the recipe.

FLUFFY MOCK CREAM

makes 2 cups

Combine 2 tablespoons milk, ¹⁄₃ cup water and 1 cup caster sugar in small saucepan; stir over low heat, without boiling, until sugar is dissolved. Sprinkle 1 teaspoon gelatine over extra 2 tablespoons water in cup, add to pan; stir syrup until gelatine is dissolved. Cool to room temperature. Beat 250g softened butter and ½ teaspoon vanilla extract in small bowl with electric mixer until as white as possible. While motor is operating, gradually pour in cold syrup; beat until light and fluffy. Mixture will thicken on standing.

tips This frosting is whiter, lighter and fluffier than butter cream, and colours better, too. Use any extract or essence you like to flavour the frosting.

FROSTINGS & ICINGS

CREAM CHEESE FROSTING

makes 1¼ cups

Beat 30g softened butter and 80g softened cream cheese in small bowl with electric mixer until light and fluffy; gradually beat in 1½ cups sifted icing sugar.

tips For a citrus flavour, beat 2 teaspoons finely grated orange, lemon or lime rind with the butter and cream cheese. This frosting goes particularly well with carrot and banana cakes. Like butter cream, it is very user-friendly, but it takes colourings slightly better than butter cream.

DARK CHOCOLATE GANACHE

makes 1 cup

Bring ½ cup cream to the boil in small saucepan; remove from heat. When bubbles subside, add 200g coarsely chopped dark eating chocolate; stir until smooth.

tip Ganache can be used while still warm and pourable, or it can be beaten with a wooden spoon until spreadable. If you want the ganache lighter and fluffier, beat the cooled mixture in a small bowl with an electric mixer.

variations
milk chocolate Replace dark eating chocolate with 200g coarsely chopped milk eating chocolate.
white chocolate Replace dark eating chocolate with 360g coarsely chopped white eating chocolate.

DAIRY-FREE CHOCOLATE FROSTING

makes ¾ cup

Combine 50g dairy-free spread, 2 tablespoons water and ¼ cup caster sugar in small saucepan; stir over low heat until sugar dissolves. Combine ¾ cup sifted pure icing sugar and 2 tablespoons cocoa powder in medium bowl; gradually stir in hot spread mixture until smooth. Cover; refrigerate 20 minutes. Using a wooden spoon, beat frosting until spreadable.

tip This frosting is easy to handle, rich and luscious, and perfect for people who can't tolerate dairy products. It's a good substitute for ganache.

GLACÉ ICING

makes 1 cup

Sift 2 cups icing sugar into small heatproof bowl; stir in 1 teaspoon butter and enough hot water (approximately 2 tablespoons) to make a thick paste. Place bowl over small saucepan of simmering water; stir until icing is spreadable.

tip It's important that the icing only be warm, not hot, while it's being stirred over the pan of water – it will crystallise if over-heated.

variations
chocolate Sift 2 teaspoons cocoa powder with the sugar.
coffee Dissolve 1 teaspoon instant coffee granules in the water.
passionfruit Stir 1 tablespoon passionfruit pulp into the mixture.

ALLSPICE also known as pimento or jamaican pepper; so-named because is tastes like a combination of nutmeg, cumin, clove and cinnamon – all spices.

ALMONDS flat, pointy-ended nuts with pitted brown shell enclosing a creamy white kernel that is covered by a brown skin.

blanched nuts with skins removed.

flaked paper-thin slices.

ground also known as almond meal; nuts are powdered to a coarse flour-like texture.

slivered flat lengthways-cut pieces.

BICARBONATE OF SODA also known as baking or carb soda.

BUTTER use salted or unsalted (sweet) butter; 125g is equal to one stick (4 ounces) of butter.

unsalted butter, often called "sweet" butter, simply has no added salt. It is mainly used in baking, and if the recipe calls for unsalted butter, then it should not be substituted.

CARAMEL TOP 'N' FILL a caramel filling made from milk and cane sugar. Can be used straight from the can for tarts, cheesecakes and slices. Has similar qualities to sweetened condensed milk, only a thicker, caramel consistency.

CHOCOLATE

choc Bits also known as chocolate chips and chocolate morsels. Made of cocoa liquor, cocoa butter, sugar and an emulsifier; these hold their shape in baking.

chocolate Melts are discs of compounded dark chocolate ideal for melting and moulding.

dark eating also known as semi-sweet or luxury chocolate; made of a high percentage of cocoa liquor and cocoa butter, and a little added sugar. Unless stated otherwise, we use dark eating chocolate in this book.

freckles chocolate discs covered with hundreds and thousands.

milk the most popular eating chocolate, mild and very sweet; similar in make-up to dark with the difference being the addition of milk solids.

chocolate-hazelnut spread we use Nutella. Originally developed when chocolate was in short supply during World War 2, so hazelnuts were added to increase supply.

rainbow chocolate chips tiny dark chocolate chips covered with a crisp sugar coating in many colours.

white eating contains no cocoa solids but derives its sweet flavour from cocoa butter. Is very sensitive to heat.

CINNAMON dried inner bark of the shoots of the cinnamon tree; available in stick (quill) or ground form.

CLOVES dried flower buds of a tropical tree; can be used whole or in ground form. Has a distinctively pungent and "spicy" scent and flavour.

COCOA POWDER also known as cocoa; dried, unsweetened, roasted then ground cocoa beans (cacao seeds).

COCONUT

desiccated unsweetened, concentrated, dried, finely shredded coconut.

flaked dried, flaked, coconut flesh.

shredded long thin strips of dried coconut.

CORN FLAKES commercially manufactured cereal made of dehydrated then baked crisp flakes of corn.

CORNFLOUR also known as cornstarch; used as a thickening agent. Available as 100% corn (maize) and wheaten cornflour.

CORN SYRUP a thick, sweet syrup created by processing cornstarch; comes in light or dark forms. Light corn syrup has been clarified to remove all colour and cloudiness; dark corn syrup, which has caramel flavour and colouring added to it, has a deeper colour and stronger flavour.

CRANBERRIES, DRIED they have the same slightly sour, succulent flavour as fresh cranberries. Available in most supermarkets.

CREAM we used fresh cream, unless otherwise stated. Also known as pure cream and pouring cream; has no additives unlike commercially thickened cream. Minimum fat content 35%.

thickened a whipping cream with 35% minimum fat content.

CREAM CHEESE commonly known as Philadelphia or Philly, a soft cows'-milk cheese with a fat content of at least 33%.

GLOSSARY

CREAM OF TARTAR the acid ingredient in baking powder; added to confectionery mixtures to help prevent sugar from crystallising. Keeps frostings creamy and improves volume when beating egg whites.

CURRANTS dried tiny, almost black raisins so-named after a grape variety that originated in Corinth, Greece.

CUSTARD POWDER instant mixture used to make pouring custard; similar to North American instant pudding mixes.

DATES fruit of the date palm tree, eaten fresh or dried, on their own or in prepared dishes. About 4cm to 6cm in length, oval and plump, thin-skinned, with a honey-sweet flavour and sticky texture.

FLOUR
plain an all-purpose flour made from wheat.
rice a very fine flour made from ground white rice.
self-raising plain flour sifted with baking powder in the proportion of 1 cup flour to 2 teaspoons baking powder.
wholemeal flour milled from whole wheat grain (bran, germ and endosperm). Available as plain or self-raising.

FOOD COLOURING dyes that can be used to change the colour of various foods.

GELATINE three teaspoons of powdered gelatine (8g or one sachet) is roughly equivalent to four gelatine leaves.

GINGER, GROUND also known as powdered ginger; cannot be substituted for fresh ginger.

glacé ginger is made from fresh ginger root preserved in sugar syrup. Crystallised ginger can be substituted if rinsed with warm water then dried.

GLACÉ CHERRIES also called candied cherries; these are boiled in a heavy sugar syrup, then dried. Found in health food stores and supermarkets.

GLACÉ ORANGES are slices of orange preserved in a sugar syrup. Found in health food stores and some of the larger supermarkets.

GOLDEN SYRUP a by-product of refined sugarcane; honey can be substituted.

HAZELNUTS also known as filberts; plump, grape-size, rich, sweet nut having a brown inedible skin that is removed by rubbing heated nuts together vigorously in a tea towel.
hazelnuts, ground have been ground into a course or fine powder. Also known as hazelnut meal.

JAM also known as preserve or conserve; most often made from fruit.

JERSEY CARAMELS two layers of sweet condensed milk caramel sandwiching a layer of white caramel. Soft, chewy and sweet.

LICORICE ALLSORTS layers of licorice sandwiched between layers of coloured fondant.

MALTED MILK POWDER a combination of wheat flour, malt flour and milk, which are evaporated to give the powder its fine appearance and to make it easily absorbable in liquids.

MANDARIN small, loose-skinned citrus fruit that is also known as tangerine.

MARMALADE a preserve, usually based on citrus fruit.

MARZIPAN an almond and sugar paste used to ice cakes and other pastries or sculpted into a variety of shapes to be eaten as candy or used as decorations.

MILK
full-cream milk powder an evaporated pasteurised milk concentrate, containing about 40% milk solids, is dried to reduce the moisture content to about 3% and prevent particles from clumping together.
sweetened condensed milk has had 60% of the water removed; the remaining milk is then sweetened with sugar.

MIXED DRIED FRUIT combination of sultanas, raisins, currants, mixed peel and cherries.

MIXED SPICE a blend of ground spices – usually cinnamon, allspice and nutmeg.

NUTMEG the dried nut of an evergreen tree native to Indonesia; it is available in ground form or you can grate your own with a fine grater.

OATS
quick cooking oats are generally thinner than rolled oats, so absorb more water and cook faster; they are thicker than "instant" oats.
rolled oats are oat groats (oats that have been husked) steamed-softened, flattened with rollers, dried and then packaged for consumption as a cereal product.

ORANGE BLOSSOM WATER also known as orange flower water; a concentrated flavouring made from orange blossoms. Available from Middle-Eastern food stores and some major supermarkets and delis. Can not be substituted with citrus flavourings, as the taste is completely different.

PASSIONFRUIT also known as granadilla; a small tropical fruit, native to Brazil, comprised of a tough outer skin surrounding edible black sweet-sour seeds. Six large passionfruit give about ½ cup of pulp.

PASTRY
  ready-rolled puff packaged sheets of frozen puff pastry, available from supermarkets.
  ready-rolled shortcrust packaged sheets of shortcrust pastry (sweet or savoury), available from supermarkets.

PEANUT BUTTER peanuts are ground to a paste; available in crunchy and smooth varieties.

PEANUTS not, in fact, a nut but the pod of a legume.

PECANS native to the United States and now grown locally; a golden-brown, buttery rich nut.

PISTACHIO pale green, delicately flavoured nut inside hard off-white shells. To peel, soak shelled nuts in boiling water for about 5 minutes; drain, then pat dry with absorbent paper. Rub skins with cloth to peel.

POLENTA also known as cornmeal; a flour-like cereal made of dried corn (maize) sold ground in different textures (from fine to coarse).

PUMPKIN SEED KERNELS also known as pepitas.

ROLLED OATS, see oats

ROSEWATER distilled from rose petals, and used in the Middle East, North Africa, and India to flavour desserts. Don't confuse this with rose essence, which is more concentrated.

SUGAR
  caster also known as superfine or finely granulated table sugar.
  dark brown a moist, dark brown sugar with a rich distinctive full flavour coming from natural molasses syrup.
  demerara small-grained golden-coloured crystal sugar.
  light brown an extremely soft, finely granulated sugar retaining molasses for its characteristic colour and flavour.
  icing sugar also known as confectioners' sugar or powdered sugar; granulated sugar crushed together with a small amount of cornflour.
  icing sugar, pure also known as confectioners' sugar or powdered sugar, but has no added cornflour.
  white a coarse, granulated table sugar, also known as crystal sugar.

SULTANAS dried grapes, also known as golden raisins.

SUNFLOWER SEED KERNELS sunflower kernels from dried husked sunflower seeds.

SWEETENED CONDENSED MILK, see milk.

TREACLE a concentrated sugar syrup with a distinctive flavour and dark black colour.

VANILLA
  beans dried long, thin pod from a tropical golden orchid grown in Central and South America and Tahiti; the minuscule black seeds inside the bean are used to impart a luscious vanilla flavour in baking and desserts. Beans can be added to caster sugar to give it a lovely vanilla flavour.
  extract made by pulping chopped vanilla beans with a mixture of alcohol and water. This gives a very strong solution, and only a couple of drops are needed to flavour most dishes.
  paste made from vanilla bean extract, vanilla bean seeds, sugar and natural thickeners. Can be used as a substitute for vanilla bean.

VEGETABLE OIL sourced from plants rather than animals.

WALNUTS the fruit of the walnut tree, which grows in temperate zones throughout the world; is rich and flavourful. Should be stored in the refrigerator because of its high oil content.

WHEAT GERM is where the seed germinates to form the sprout that becomes wheat. The term "germ" comes from the word germinate. It has a nutty flavour and is very oily, which causes it to turn rancid quickly. Wheat germ is usually separated from the bran and starch during the milling of flour because its perishable oil content limits the keeping time of the flour. It is available from health-food stores and supermarkets.

CONVERSION CHART

MEASURES

One Australian metric measuring cup holds approximately 250ml, one Australian metric tablespoon holds 20ml, one Australian metric teaspoon holds 5ml.

The difference between one country's measuring cups and another's is within a 2- or 3-teaspoon variance, and will not affect your cooking results. North America, New Zealand and the United Kingdom use a 15ml tablespoon. All cup and spoon measurements are level. The most accurate way of measuring dry ingredients is to weigh them. When measuring liquids, use a clear glass or plastic jug with metric markings.

We use large eggs with an average weight of 60g.

DRY MEASURES

METRIC	IMPERIAL
15g	½oz
30g	1oz
60g	2oz
90g	3oz
125g	4oz (¼lb)
155g	5oz
185g	6oz
220g	7oz
250g	8oz (½lb)
280g	9oz
315g	10oz
345g	11oz
375g	12oz (¾lb)
410g	13oz
440g	14oz
470g	15oz
500g	16oz (1lb)
750g	24oz (1½lb)
1kg	32oz (2lb)

LIQUID MEASURES

METRIC	IMPERIAL
30ml	1 fluid oz
60ml	2 fluid oz
100ml	3 fluid oz
125ml	4 fluid oz
150ml	5 fluid oz (¼ pint)
190ml	6 fluid oz
250ml	8 fluid oz
300ml	10 fluid oz (½ pint)
500ml	16 fluid oz
600ml	20 fluid oz (1 pint)
1000ml (1 litre)	1¾ pints

LENGTH MEASURES

METRIC	IMPERIAL
3mm	⅛in
6mm	¼in
1cm	½in
2cm	¾in
2.5cm	1in
5cm	2in
6cm	2½in
8cm	3in
10cm	4in
13cm	5in
15cm	6in
18cm	7in
20cm	8in
23cm	9in
25cm	10in
28cm	11in
30cm	12in (1ft)

OVEN TEMPERATURES

These oven temperatures are only a guide for conventional ovens. For fan-forced ovens, check the manufacturer's manual.

	°C (CELSIUS)	°F (FAHRENHEIT)	GAS MARK
Very slow	120	250	½
Slow	150	275-300	1-2
Moderately slow	160	325	3
Moderate	180	350-375	4-5
Moderately hot	200	400	6
Hot	220	425-450	7-8
Very hot	240	475	9

INDEX

Published in 2010 by ACP Books, Sydney
ACP Books are published by ACP Magazines
a division of PBL Media Pty Limited

ACP BOOKS

General manager Christine Whiston
Editor-in-chief Susan Tomnay
Creative director Hieu Chi Nguyen
Art director Hannah Blackmore
Designer Sarah Holmes
Senior editor Wendy Bryant
Food director Pamela Clark

Sales & rights director Brian Cearnes
Marketing manager Bridget Cody
Senior business analyst Rebecca Varela
Circulation manager Jama Mclean
Operations manager David Scotto
Production manager Victoria Jefferys

Published by ACP Books, a division of
ACP Magazines Ltd, 54 Park St, Sydney;
GPO Box 4088, Sydney, NSW 2001.
phone (02) 9282 8618; fax (02) 9267 9438.
acpbooks@acpmagazines.com.au;
www.acpbooks.com.au

Printed by Toppan Printing Co., China.

United Kingdom Distributed by Australian Consolidated Press (UK),
phone (01604) 642 200; fax (01604) 642 300; books@acpuk.com

Title: Baking favourites / food director Pamela Clark.
ISBN: 978 186396 929 1 (pbk.)
Notes: Includes index.
Subjects: Baking. Confectionery. Cookery.
Other Authors/Contributors: Clark, Pamela.
Dewey Number: 641.815

© ACP Magazines Ltd 2010
ABN 18 053 273 546

Cover Cherry and sultana buttercake, page 59
Photographer Tanya Zouev
Stylist Vicki Liley
Food preparation Ariarne Bradshaw

Send recipe enquiries to: recipeenquiries@acpmagazines.com.au